Love Is Straight from the Heart

A Book of Poetry

by

Diana "Lynn" Byrd

DORRANCE PUBLISHING CO., INC.
PITTSBURGH, PENNSYLVANIA 15222

This is a work of fiction. Names, characters, places, and incidents are either the product of the author's imagination or are used fictitiously, and any resemblance to actual persons, living or dead, or locales, is entirely coincidental.

All Rights Reserved
Copyright © 1998 by Diana "Lynn" Byrd
No part of this book may be reproduced or transmitted in any form or by any means, electronic or mechanical, including photocopying, recording, or by any information storage and retrieval system without permission in writing from the publisher.

ISBN # 0-8059-3993-8
Printed in the United States of America

Second Printing

For information or to order additional books, please write:
Dorrance Publishing Co., Inc.
643 Smithfield Street
Pittsburgh, Pennsylvania 15222
U.S.A.

Dedication

I would like to dedicate my book to my father, Reverend Ernest Byrd. When I was very young, my father would let me rewrite his sermons for him, and he would read from my manuscript handwriting. A few years later, my father was killed in an automobile accident. It was through that depressing time in my life I started writing poetry. There is one specific poem written in memory of my father. The poem is entitled "On the Other Side." This is the message my father left with me to share with others. He is my guardian angel. I know he had to leave this world in order to make it a better place for me.

Contents

A Tribute: Ernestine Byrd Anderson 1
My Dedication 3
On the Other Side 4
Our Family 5
Thanks for Your Prayers 7
Just As You Are 8
You're Not Alone 9
The Flame 10
You Will Find Peace 11
Friends for Life 12
He's Coming Back Again 13
We Are Family 14
Especially for You: Sister Mary Louise Burton 15
Mother's Day 17
Happy Mother's Day 18
The Joy That Thanksgiving Brings 19
Count Your Blessings 20
Happy Easter Day 21
Maya Angelou 22
A Tribute: Dr. Martin Luther King, Jr. .23
Today the Occasion Is: Black History,
    Which Was Founded by Dr. Carter G. Woodson 24
The Night We Met Sinbad 25
My Success Is on Its Way 27
Believe in Your Dreams 28
Love Is 29

Perfect World	30
Sometimes I Sit and Think	31
I Love You	32
Under the Moonlight	33
Thinking of You	34
At the End of the Rainbow	35
I've Always Wanted	36
We're Lucky	37
I Wish	38
I Need You	39
You Told Me	40
Only You	41
I Would Like To	42
Have You Ever	43
Yes, I Have Always Wished For	44
Face-to-Face	45
Best Friends	46
This Time	48
Your Smiling Face	49
Love Is Not Enough	50
Have I Told You Lately I Love You	51
There Comes a Time	52
I'm Hurting Inside	53
If Our Love Was Meant to Be	54
For the Two of You to Share	55
The Cotton Field	56
The Desert Floor	57
To the Athlete	58
Creative Arts in Learning	59
A Montessori Child Is the Future of Tomorrow	60
I Quit	61
If It Is to Be, It's Up to Me	62
Physical Education Song, Repeat After Me	63

Acknowledgments

I would like to acknowledge my Heavenly Father, for He is the head of my life. I want to thank Him for His many blessings, His strength, His guidance, and His wisdom. He is the superior giver of love, and He has given that precious love to me. In return I'm going to share it with others unconditionally. I would like to acknowledge my dear mother, Ernestine Byrd Anderson, who inspired me to be the very best I can be; my stepfather, Alvin Anderson, who has stood by my mother's side; my sister, Dedtra; my brother, Tyrone; my grandmother, Carrie, who is the backbone of our family; as well as my nieces, nephews, relatives, and my friends.

A Tribute
Ernestine Byrd Anderson

Born to this world, on the ninth day of June, some years ago,
A very special lady, who we have grown to love so,
A very caring parent, mother, and friend,
Who gave birth to three children: Dedtra, Tyrone, and Lynn.

Today we tribute her, on this very special day,
Letting her know we love her in a very special way.
We thank her for her gratitude, her loyalty, and her love,
And may God bless her from Heaven above.

Her struggle wasn't easy as she started her road to success,
She paved the way for us to follow in her footsteps.
She kept good care of us, and she stayed close by our side,
And our love for our dear mother we can't hide.

She put a roof over our heads and gave us food to eat,
And she kept clothes on our little bodies and shoes on our feet.
She taught us to pray each and every day, and every night,
She taught us praying would someday show us the light,

She taught us God could make mountains out of molehills,
And whatever He wished would be His will.
And He doesn't make mistakes, no matter what he does,
And we must always put Him first in whatever we do.

We love you with all our hearts, and we hope your birthday
   wishes come true,
One of our wishes has already come true
Because our most precious gift in this world is you.
We tribute you, Mom, on your very special day,
We wish you happiness as each day passes away.

May God bless you to see another birthday.
He has blessed our family in each and every way.
For your outstanding job with us and the hard work you do,
From Dedtra, Lynn, Tyrone, and your grandchildren too.
From all of us. Have a happy birthday, and we love you.

My Dedication

This book with my first poem is dedicated to you, Mother, who I love so dear,
And to only you, my dear Mother, I will always be near,
You have inspired me to be the very best I can be,
You taught me to stay close to God and a brighter day I will see.

Which shines deep down in my soul within,
And only you, dear Mother, I can always depend,
Mother, you are my Africa Queen,
And no words can express just what I mean,
Out of all the other mothers, you are simply the very best.

Mother, you are loving and very unique,
And you will always be a soldier for Christ by the holy words you speak,
Mother, you have given me joy and love, and you have kept hope alive,
And you taught me to pray each day the sun does set and rise.

You work so very hard, and in each and every day,
And yes, Mother, you will wear your golden crown in Heaven some day,
I could go on and on about what you mean to me,
If it wasn't for you, where oh where would I be.

You have given me more love than many others will ever see,
I just wish others could feel the love which flows from you to me,
Mother, this is just the first of many poems, I want to dedicate to you,
For your outstanding commitment, thanks Mother, for making your baby's dreams come true

On the Other Side

When we're born to this world, surely we must die
And to all my family, friends, and love ones, it's alright to cry
God has blessed me with the finest family and friends in this great land.
And now I'm going home, with my God to hold my hands.

I'm glad I had a chance to live my life where there was so much love.
And now I'm going home to live with my God in Heaven above.
So to all my family, friends, and loved ones, take one day at a time
And always keep the joyous memories of me in your minds.

And one day we will meet again, on the other side
But for now, my friends, I must close my eyes
I'm in a peaceful resting place everyone will someday see
For we know this is God's will
Someday for you, but now for me

The memories we've shared will always be near to your hearts
And there they will stay and never depart
But for now, my friends, I must close my eyes
And one day we will meet again, on the other side.

Our Family

We are decedents of the parent race, Africa; we were
 transported to a new land,
And brought to this country many, many years ago by an
 unjust man,
But through it all, we kept the faith, and God, He saw us
 through,
And we were able to trace back to our ancestors' roots.

We claimed our songs, we claimed our dance, among all
 other things,
But most of all, we were able to fall down on our knees,
To give thanks to our heavenly Father, for blessing us each
day.
He gave strength and courage to our forefathers and mothers;
 for us they paved the way.

Our culture and our heritage will enable us to move forward,
 and never back,
And we must never bow down to anyone just because our
 faces are black,
And we must never forget it was our ancestors who built this
world, in which we live,
They healed the sick, educated the ignorant, and gave
wisdom to our women and men.

We are all God's creation, and we each have a purpose in
 His world,
And our future is in the hands of the children, our little boys
 and girls,
We must be role models for our offspring, they are the next
 generation,
So they will be proud to lay a strong and solid foundation.

To become doctors, lawyers, preachers, and even teachers too,
To follow their dreams and we must help make their dreams
   come true,
We must all remember the Lord, He is is our Shepherd,
   leading our journey's way,
And surely and goodness will follow us, each and every day.

So, Family, tonight, before I take my seat,
I would like each and everyone to stand on their feet,
I would like everyone to turn around, look around, to see,
Just how far the Lord has brought our family.

For the Brown-Pickett-Johnson Family Reunion
June 23-25, 1995 in Houston, Texas.
God bless you all.

Thanks for Your Prayers

I would like to thank you for thinking of me in my time
   of sorrow
And one thing is for certain, we are not promised tomorrow.
My uncle was a soldier for Christ, and he was called home to
   hold His hand,
And one day, you and I will look over that Promised Land.

As I read this card, a pleasant feeling came over me
I know whatever will be will be; the future is not ours to see.
I believe the Lord will love and keep me from all hurt, harm,
   and pain
And a stronger heart I will gain.

Thanks for your prayers; they mean so very much,
And thanks for the card, my heart is truly touched,
Lastly, I just would like to thank you again for your thoughts
   and prayers in my difficult time.
May the Lord bless you and keep you until the end of time.

Just As You Are

God's love will be the same each and every day
He will never stop loving His creation, no mater what
   others say.
And to him it doesn't matter the color of your skin.
God loves you, and upon Him you can always depend.

No matter what others tell you, or how they beat you down
To Him it doesn't matter, if your face is white, pale, or brown.
As sure as the sun and moon shine, as far as the eye can see
God's love is everlasting, and He will love you through all
   eternity.

For all the names and labels others may give
Just keep the faith and do His will
For He said if you take one step, He would take two
He will never forsake you no matter what others do

Just steal away and call on His Holy Name
Take your burdening to the Lord, He knows all your pain
He will fill your heart with love and peace, and you will
   go far
Because God loves all His children, just as you are

You're Not Alone

There comes a time in everyone's life when reality sets in.
And the arts of real life and real feelings begin.
And to lose a beloved one becomes a surprise,
As we are left with tears of sadness in our eyes.

But no one is at fault, and no one is to blame,
Although we know the world will never be the same
Because that special person brought love and joy to our life.
Now to keep on going is a true sacrifice.

Now spending time alone, thinking of the past
Knowing those special memories will always last
To know you can smile again, remembering the good times
And those special moments together will always be in mind.

The special memories, shared, can never be taken away,
They will make you stronger as each day passes away,
Just keep your hand in God's hand, and He will see you
    through,
And put your trust in Him and remember He loves you.

No one knows what the future holds but the good Lord
    up above
And to all His children, He will spread His love.
He will watch over our beloved ones, as He calls them home
Because with Him is where they truly belong.

Doing His will, because mistakes He makes, none
Calling our beloved ones on home, one by one.
And in the end, we will all meet in heaven, our new home.
But remember, for now, you're not alone.

The Flame

By the candlelight, you sit with countless confusions on
  your mind,
Wondering of many, many things, you've done in your time,
As you watch the dance of the flame, with a calm eye,
Knowing God is looking down on you from on high.

As the sweet candle flickers in the darkness, so very clear,
You feel the warm presence of your Savior near,
You feel His arms around you, Oh so tight,
As you look deep into the candlelight.

Dance for me, dance for me, you say, so soft and so sweet,
And the flicker of the flame will let you see,
Into your soul, into your soul, so deep,
And your soul, He will always keep,
The flame will never leave you alone,
Because in your soul is where it belongs.

God is the flame inside of you,
As it flickers to you, He will always be true,
And when your flame burns down, just call His Holy Name,
And He will give you back the flame.

You Will Find Peace

There are so many things I want to say,
About how I feel, in each and every way,
I want to commend you on your unique style, and
 compassion too,
For being a wonderful mother, and to a friend you are true,

You are very close to your family and your friends,
You stick with them through thick and thin,
Your deep-down feelings you try to hold inside,
And you are always doing for them when you are too tired,

I know you've been through ups and downs in the past,
And you wanted the relationship to always last,
But you will get stronger as you pray by candlelight,
And God will make everything all right.

For you to do the things you have always wanted to do,
Just put your trust in Him and He will aid you,
I know at times it seems so hard to bear,
And sometimes it seems life is not fair,

But you must not forget, God will take good care of you,
Just keep your faith in Him, no matter what you do,
And remember, take only one day at a time,
And love, joy, and most of all peace, you will find.

Friends for Life

From the first moment I met you, I knew you would be,
A very special and dear friend to me,
I find myself thinking about the day we first met,
And it was a memorable moment, I will never forget.

You are a very special friend, special in many many ways,
And I will treasure our friendship for always,
God has brought us together to share our joys and love,
And we will forever give thanks to our Father in heaven above,

I feel God our Father has a special purpose for us in His world.
And some day we will walk with Him through His gates of pearls.

We will sing songs of praise and never get tired in Heaven our new home,
Because with our Father is where His children belong,
I can't thank Him enough for sending me a very special friend,
And a friend for life is who you have in Diana Lynn,

May God bless you and keep near, in each and every way,
And may He give you strength and courage, each and every day,
As you go out into this world, speaking His Holy word,
To His sheep, and to the sinners, His word will be heard.

This special friendship was truly brought together by the good Lord up above,
And each day we live, we will spread His most precious love,
And very very special friends for life we will always be,
This poem was composed especially for you by me.

He's Coming Back Again

He's coming back again, and it will be sometime soon,
No one knows whether it will be in the morning or at noon.
Make sure you're ready to meet your maker at this time so
you won't be committed for an eternal crime.

He's coming back for those who obeyed the golden rules,
But to those who didn't, their lives they will lose.
Of course you still have to get your life intact,
But you better not take too long, cause he's coming back.

There are some who go to church to show off their pretty
   clothes,
Your pastor, family, and friends may not know who you are,
   but the Lord knows
Fine clothes, fine cars, and money won't get you on His train,
So get your life together, cause He's coming back again.

Don't take my word for it, just read the good book,
And just like me, you too will also get hooked.
This can be a fresh start and not a bad end.
Get your life in order, cause He's coming back again.

We Are Family

S- econd Baptist Church is a place one can come to worship and pray
E- ach and every one is welcome, so come enjoy your stay
C- ome and visit with us, we're known for our down-home hospitality.
O- ur members will welcome you with open arms into our family
N- ever hesitate to ask for prayers or counseling of some kind,
D- oors are open to you and yours during your most troubled times.

B- ring your heart and soul to the Lord, He will never turn you away
A- lways remember to keep your hand in His hand each and every day.
P- lease join in with us and sing a hymn from the days of old
T- old by our forefathers bearing their heavy load
I- n our Father's house we worship in harmony,
S- inging and praising His name simultaneously.
T- idings and offerings are both part of our Father's will.

C- ome and bring forth, we thank those who gave and those who didn't have it to give.
H- umble yourself before the Lord of all the land,
U- nconditional Love from God our Father and from us unto our fellow man.
R- eceiving salvation from our Lord Savior Jesus Christ,
C- omfort and strength is found in this place.
H- allelujah! hallelujah! is the highest praise in our Father's House.

Especially for You: Sister Mary Burton

I would like to take this time to personally thank you,
For all your wisdom, your knowledge, and the hard work you do,
I know you are a soldier for Christ, and you are truly blessed,
And to me, you're simply the very best.

I was sent to your class by the good Lord up above,
And for all of his blessings unto me, I will forever spread my love.
As you speak on the Bible lesson, I'm closed in my right mind,
And any time the lesson is on our Savior, that's a very good sign.

Teachers are very special people, special in many ways,
You are the ones who mold us by the things you do and say,
You also teach love and kindness unto your fellow man,
And teachers are very dedicated to the subject at hand.

Each teacher has different qualities, their methods aren't quite the same,
But they all want to instill a message in their student's brains,
Their guidance is important, and their wisdom is too,
I'm very glad I have a Sunday school teacher like you.

The message that teach, God is the way,
The message that teach, we must pray each day,
The message that teach, if you're down and out and don't know what to do,
Take your burdens to the Lord, and He will aid you.

Your past experiences and examples of what you bring to us are true,
But you kept the faith and you know for sure God loves you,
Now your walk in faith, your rewards bring happiness, and you are free,
And you only take one day at a time, and that's how it should be.

We know God is good all the time, and He will love us through all eternity,
And He will watch over us, as we rise and even as we sleep,
May the Lord keep blessing you, and to Him you will always be near,
Because to his children you are so kind and so very dear.

I want to thank you from the bottom of my heart for being so special to me,
Because there is an abundance of knowledge, wisdom, and understanding of the Bible lessons in you I see,
You have definitely made an impact on me, and I wanted to tell you,
And with the grace of God, I will make the same impact on my students too.

Teachers are a special grade of people in a class by themselves.

Mother's Day

M-ay I share a few words with you
O-f some of the special things mothers do
T- his is your day, so what shall it be,
H- ow about sitting down and relaxing your feet
E- veryone loves Mom, although they may not say,
R- emembering mothers are their very best friend
S- he will be there, through thick and thin
D- on't worry about anything. Mom, we'll be there for you
A- nd make you smile, when you're feeling blue,
Y- ou're a very special mother, as special as can be.

Happy Mother's Day

Mother's Day is here again, so what shall it be?
If you are not sure here are a few suggestions from me:
Would you like your family to wait on you hand and foot?
Or would you rather curl up in bed and read a good book?
Would you like to sleep in and have breakfast in bed?
Or would you rather have a quiet morning to yourself
   instead?

It's up to only you, so make up your mind, mothers have
   only one day;
You don't have a lot of time.
Would you like to go shopping for that special little outfit?
Or would you rather be surprised when you open your gift?
Would you like to go for a short drive to a very quiet place?
Or would you rather your children bring a smile to your face?

Would you like to eat your favorite candies, cakes, and
   sweets?
Or would you rather your family prepare your special
   Mother's Day feast?
This day is set aside for all mothers, so make your special
   wishes known today,
And let your family and friends share in your happiness in
   every way.

You have been blessed to see another Mother's Day and to
   have your health and strength too,
And always remember your family loves you.
This Mother's Day I hope your Mother's Day wishes come
   true!
Have a happy, happy, Mother's Day from me to you

The Joy That Thanksgiving Brings

Thanksgiving Day is a day set aside to thank the Lord for from which you have come,
The family must all get together and praise Him for all He has done.
For giving us a chance to all meet on another Thanksgiving Day,
To have our family and friends home in a special and glorious way.

Families have come from far and near to give thanks to heaven above,
They come with joy in their hearts and plenty of warmth and love.
A big dinner is always prepared on this Thanksgiving Day,
And everyone gives thanks in their own loving way.

Some may thank Him for bringing them from a mighty, mighty long way,
And others may thank Him for letting them see another brand new day.
Always trust in Him and take only one day at a time,
And with Him peace, joy, and love your family will find.

Thank Him for His many, many blessings, His love is here to stay,
Just don't thank Him on this day but each and every other day,
I hope this poem has brightened this family on this glorious holiday,
And I wish this family many, many happy days in a Thanksgiving way.

Count Your Blessings

Count your blessings, for there is someone worse off than you,
Others have problems, they too don't know what to do,
Christmas is the time for giving one's love,
And always give thanks to Heaven above.

Giving from the heart is a blessing in itself,
I'm sure you have given until there was nothing left.
Count your blessings, for you will be blessed in some way,
Don't count them only at Christmas but each and every day.

The Lord said, "If you take one step, He will take two,"
Just count your blessings, and your wishes may come true,
Everyone has one wish they want fulfilled this year,
And my wish is for you and yours to be blessed so dear.

I will always love this family with my heart, soul, and mind,
Just keep counting your blessings and peace, joy, and love you will find,
For it is this family my heart will always be near,
I wish you and yours a very Merry Christmas and a very Happy New Year.

Happy Easter Day

H- ail to the King, Easter is finally here,
A- wonderful time to spread some cheer,
P- eople young, and people old, will praise His holy name,
P- raising Jesus, Who hung and died in pain.
Y- ou have this day to give praise to your King,

E- aster is the time to lift every voice and sing,
A- nd we must not forget the stone which was rolled away,
S- o we all could have eternal life some day.
T- ruly this day shall bring you happiness and much joy,
E- very women, man, girl, and every boy,
R- emember Easter, in your very own loving way,

D- on't forget for whom the stone was rolled away.
A- nd there is one other thing I'd like to say
Y- ou and yours, have a happy, happy Easter day.

Maya Angelou

When you hear the name Maya Angelou, you first think of
   wisdom and knowledge and then of love.
And one thing's for certain: She always gave thanks to
   Heaven above.
For letting her travel around the world and back.
And the words from her lips were not fiction but facts.

She spoke to many people, from every color of the rainbow.
This very unique lady of whom I speak highly is
   Maya Angelou.
With her soft voice, with a very positive tone, for all to hear.
And the powerful words she speaks would make the strongest
   of eyes tear.

Her memories and her poetry have inspired numerous young
   Americans to be all they could be.
With the belief that no obstacles or barriers will deprive me.
Of my freedom, of my self-esteem, or my self-confidence,
Or my self-worth, my pride, or even my intelligence.

As she reads from the steps of the capital, the poem entitled
   "On the Pulse of the Morning,"
In hope to bring the world together for a new beginning.
To plant the seed of hope for the survival and betterment of
   all those like her,
Her prayer was that others would know themselves better by
   reading what she wrote.

In closing, I would like to leave you with this note:
For a new beginning, one must remember their past to be
   able to create a future
And one must always trust and have faith in Our Heavenly
   Father, Who sits high and looks low,
And you too my friend will be a phenomenal individual like
   Maya Angelou.

A Tribute: Dr. Martin Luther King, Jr.

Dr. Martin Luther King's birthday is now a national holiday for us all.
Our race has come a long way and now we can stand tall,
Dr. King was killed for speaking up for what he knew was right,
There were some who didn't want to make his birthday a holiday, but we won the fight.

He has done so much for the brothers and sisters all over this great land,
Dr. King was a Nobel Peace Prize winner and a hell of a man,
The Lord gave him the strength and courage to speak His holy word,
To every man, woman, boy, and girl his word was heard.

Dr. Martin Luther King lead the march on Washington in 1963
He helped pave the way for people like you and me.
He spoke to hundreds of thousands on non-violence and the movement of our civil rights,
He had a dream for our children—they would not struggle but would someday see the light.

That would shine so very bright, for all people to see,
Dr. King always preached love for his fellow man and equality.
And no matter what happens in the future of our land,
Dr. King put in the hearts of people a sense of "I know I can."

His struggle for freedom will always be a difficult task
But one thing is for certain, everyone will remember the speech
"I Have a Dream": ...Free at Last, Free at Last, Thank God Almighty, I'm Free at Last...."
From the man who spoke from the mountain top for all to hear,
This tribute is for you, Dr. Martin Luther King, Jr., each and every year.

Today the Occasion Is Black History, Which Was Founded by Dr. Carter G. Woodson

African-Americans have every reason to be proud of their
 heritage and the right to be free,
Dr. Carter Woodson founded the Association for the Study of
 Negro Life and History
He came to realize that the black man's past contributions
 had to be documented and taught,
And many other brothers and sisters all over this great land
 also struggled and fought.

For our people to take a stand so the whole world could see
We were all created equal, and each and every one should
 be free
Dr. Carter Woodson found that many of the achievements of
 blacks were overlooked
He made it possible for our children to read of their history
 in text books.

If a race had no recorded history, he said, "...its achievements
 would be forgotten in time...."
The Father of Black History, fought—for black America and
 all mankind
It was his dream that the truth would be revealed in each and
 every way
His prime ambition was that "...young blacks would grow up
 with a firm knowledge of their ancestors one day."

Thanks to Dr. Carter Woodson, the month of February is
 Black History Month all over the world
And black history should be taught to every boy and girl
Borrowing on Frederick Douglas's infinite wisdom, without a
 struggle there can be to progress
Black Americans, from the young to the old, each and every
 day of your life is a test.

The Night We Met Sinbad

It was on a Friday night, on which I had nothing to do,
So Margo asked me to a show on the Strip "Starring You."
And little did I know that on this particular eve,
And certainly know one could ever believe,

We would party with you, in the town that never sleeps,
And we would dance until the corns hurt on our feet,
To us, Sinbad, you are kind, gentle, and very sweet,
And a very unique person, who we were very glad to meet.

Your show was filled with happiness; laughter; and much, much more.
And you were the young man thousands of fans truly adored,
Your message was very clear, and your dialogue was true,
And the words you spoke everyone admired, and they highly respected you.

As I sat attentively with a smile on my face,
We didn't know at the moment what would take place,
We could have sat and listened to you all night,
To us, Sinbad, your show was truly a wonderful delight.

We listened as you talked about your children and how they act each day,
Hoping they would soon grow up, for them you would pray,
It was fun to see you create an act on lovers and their mate,
And how you made mention of the cowboy and the couple who were late.

And even the lady who ate too much and didn't want to leave,
And the cowboy's jeans were too tight—he couldn't breathe,
And every one in the filled room was having a good time,
And the use of profanity no one would ever find.

And when the show was over, we got a chance to go
    backstage,
And we met your sister; brother; friends; and your
    daughter, Page,
And your five-year-old son was on the couch catching a
    few ZZZZZZs.
We soon went to your suite, to catch the midnight breeze.

We made plans to go to the club just down the block,
The Club Rio, we heard, really rocked around the clock,
We would soon enter the very big room, for all eyes to see,
As the people watched you, surly they would say, "Could it
    really be?"

Some people said, "No, I really don't think,"
And others said, "Yes," and their curious eyes did blink,
As we moved across the room slowly to our seats,
Hundreds of women and men instantly you would meet.

The D.J. was spinning the wheels from the Pop-Lock days
    of olds,
To the sounds of Flash Light, Brick House, as it comforted
    our souls,
And you and I danced to the music from the good old days,
As we stepped to the tunes of Confuction and the Bar-Kays.

And soon it was time for our hugs and our goodbyes,
We still had sparkles in our eyes,
To us, Sinbad, you are by far one very stylish, class act,
And we will party again whenever you come back.

May God bless you and your family each and every day,
And may you stay closer to Him in each and every way,
I hope you have enjoyed this poem as much as I've enjoyed
    writing it for you.
And remember to always put God first in your life, in
    whatever you do.

                                    P.S. I'm a P.K. too (Preacher Kid)

My Success Is on Its Way

I was put on this earth to play a special part
And now I think it's time for me to start.
I have a special talent, to write and to rhyme,
All I have to do is to use my mind.

Success is on its way, and I'm going to do my very best,
For the people I love, I won't settle for anything less.
I've wanted all my life for this day to come,
But I must be patient; this road has just begun.

And I know it will be rough, but nothing or no one will get me down.
Now my feet are firmly on solid ground.
Yes, I've always wanted the coming of this day,
I'm happy to say my success is on its way.

Believe In Your Dreams

Believe in your dreams, for only you can make them
   come true,
The key is believing, and that's not hard to do,
Just give yourself a chance, believing is the way,
Believe in your dreams, for they may come true someday,

Your dreams are what you want, and they don't mean much
   to others,
For they are your dreams, not your sister's or your brother's
Just believe in yourself, and your dreams will fall in place,
Remember to keep your hands in God's hands and His
   good grace,

Making dreams come true is truly up to only you,
And it is something I'm sure you can do,
If in your dream you come to a brook or a stream,
Don't be afraid, cross it, and don't stop believing in
   your dreams.

Love Is

Love is like a snow white dove,
Love is a gift from Heaven above.
Love is you, and love is me,
Love is us together, as one can see.

Love is watching a little child play,
That love will last day after day,
Love is his little hands, and his little feet
Love is when he smiles back at me.

Love is that child when he knows right from wrong,
And when he grows older, he will always find his way
   back home
Love is teaching him God is the way,
And love is praying each and every day.

Yes I once was a child, and I learned how to love,
And I always give thanks to Heaven above
Loving someone is easy; it's not so hard to do,
By the way, have I told you I truly love you.

Perfect World

If this was a perfect world, everything would be great,
And there would be plenty of love and no hate,
If this was a perfect world, we could love one another.
But instead we try to kill our own brother,

A perfect world would be wonderful t live in,
But instead it is filled with hatred and sin,
We should set examples for the next young generation,
But instead we are the cause of this situation,

This world would be perfect if we could come together as one
And the hatred in it would be all gone
For united we stand and divided we fall,
This world could be perfect with the help of us all.

Sometimes I Sit and Think

Sometimes I sit and think about the heartbreaks of my past,
And how the love I once had really could have last.
In those days I thought love would never end,
But now I have to start my life all over again.

It is getting hard for me to face reality,
I don't think another love like that will ever be,
When I love, I put all of me into one, and I'm sure you do,
I want to love like that again but I'm afraid to.

My heart is very lonely, and I need a close friend,
To share my feelings and thoughts with, that I have
   locked within,
But someday I'm going to get lucky and find my missing link,
And then I won't have to sometimes just sit and think!

I Love You

Yes, I love you more than words can express,
And all of my love is yours because you deserve nothing less,
You show me you love me, and you don't have to say a word,
When you think it, your thoughts are heard.

I know it's hard to say "I love you" because you are so far away,
Just keep saying it, over and over, I will be with you someday.
I'm counting the seconds, minutes, hours, that we are apart,
And once we're back together, we will never depart.

And when our eyes meet, we will fall in love all over again,
And both of our hearts will soon mend.
So it's natural for two people to be in love,
And I will forever be your little dove.

Under the Moonlight

What a night it was under the moonlight,
The moon was full, and the stars were shining bright,
Under the moonlight is where we met,
And a night we'll never never forget.

You smiled at me as tears rolled down my face,
And we both knew a precious moment was about to
    take place.
You said you were happier than you'd ever been
And told me your love would never never end.

The stars were shining so very bright,
You asked me to marry you under the moonlight,
We walked through the woods to our secret little place,
And once I opened my eyes, a smile came to my face.

In a tent, a candlelight dinner for two,
You said, "Baby, I did this all for you,"
We toasted to you, and then to me,
You said, "You make me happy."

Under the moon is where we met,
And a night we will never forget,
You said you love me; I love you too,
And someday we're going to make this dream come true.

Thinking of You

My mind is always wandering out in space these days,
And I know this is one very serious phase.
There are things I want to tell you, that are on my mind,
But somehow I haven't found the right time.

I'm still in love with him, and we have been through so much in the past.
I guess that's why I wanted our relationship to really last.
But it's getting harder for me to be without that special someone,
And I know now something has to be done.

I don't want it to be over, but I can't hold on,
To a hope, to a dream, or to a bond.
But he will always have a special place in my heart,
I love him so much it hurts, but it's best for us to be apart.

Just being with you, and spending time,
Gives me joy, happiness, and a peace of mind.
And it's good to know, I have a friend,
And I hope our friendship will last to the end

Whatever happens in the future is something we can't change,
But our close friendship will always remain the same.
When I'm sitting alone, with nothing to do,
I know that I can smile when I'm thinking of you!

At the End of the Rainbow

At the end of the rainbow is where my treasure lay,
And I am going to get that treasure someday.
I know it will be an uphill climb to get to those goods,
But I will walk through rocks, over mountains, or even wood.

I will reach high, and I will reach low,
I will do whatever it takes to reach my rainbow,
I will keep trying, each and every day,
Because at the end of the rainbow is where my treasure lay.

Yes, it's all there, and all of it goes to me,
A very handsome young man lay at my feet.
You are at the end of my rainbow, can't you see,
And the color in it represents your love for me.

I never thought I would reach the end,
And there is where we will join hands,
I will love you forever, and my love will be true.
Did you know? At the end of my rainbow was you!

I've Always Wanted

I've always wanted to meet a person as special as you,
And tonight that wonderful dream came true.
I think a great deal of you, by the way you carry yourself,
You have a style that's very unique, unlike anyone else.

I've often listened to your songs, the words mean a lot
 to me,
Your songs give me peace of mind, and they are truly
 a reality.
God has given you the talent to sing from your heart,
And your songs will stay within me and never depart.

May God bless you and keep you so near,
And to you, He will always be dear.
Just keep your hands in His hand, and He will see
 you through,
And always remember, He loves you.

He will always be there for you, through thick and thin,
He will be there until the end.
I've always wanted to meet a special person such as you,
And tonight my dream came true.

We're Lucky

I thought to myself today, while I was alone,
Wishing I was with you in our own little home,
We're the two most luckiest people in this world,
And forever and ever, I will be your special girl.

It was faith that brought us together,
And together is where we will stay forever,
I think about how we met, and how you looked into my eyes,
And I know you were the man I wanted by my side.

When I'm with you, I feel like a lucky charm,
You are my knight, keeping me from all harm.
I love you very much, and I know you love me,
And that's why, we are so L-U-C-K-Y.

I Wish

I wish you didn't have to travel so far,
But my heart, soul, and mind will be wherever you are,
I will pray for you each and every day,
I wish you will have a safe and joyful stay.

I wish I had met you a long time ago,
For a man like you I've searched high and low.
I'm glad I'm the woman of your dreams,
We must pray every day and truly believe.

I wish our relationship will grow stronger each day.
We must keep praying, God will make a way,
May God bless and keep you until you return to me,
Because with me is where you should always be.

I Need You

I need you and want you here with me,
Together is where we both should be,
I need your special love to make my life complete,
Because you are so dear and sweet.

No matter what it takes to get back to you,
Then that is what I will do.
Yes, I need you here, although you are here in my heart,
And there is where you will be and never depart.

It won't be long until I'm by your side,
There, forever, I will be and never get tired,
And I'm sure you need and want to be with me, too,
But most of all, I want to come home to be with you.

You Told Me

You told me you love me and for me not to be afraid,
You told me your love for me would never fade away,
You told me we'd be together until the end of time,
But now I have only memories left in my mind.

You told me you would never leave me or give up,
You told me our love would be like two little pups.
You told me you would give me the stars, the moon,
  and much more,
You told me I was the lady you adored.

You also told me we'd have fun under the cherry tree,
You also told me you would never leave me.
I'm still believing that dream, which never came true,
And now I have only memories in my mind of you.

Only You

Only you can make me smile when I'm feeling blue,
Every time you look at me, I'm smiling back at you.
No one could ever take your place,
That look in your eyes brings a smile to my face.

Our love will grow stronger, day by day,
And our love will never fade away,
You have given me everything my heart desires,
My love for you is raging with fire.

Someday you will truly believe
That you are the only man for me.
I will love you till the end of time,
With the sweet memories of only you in my mind!

I Would Like To

I would like to go with you somewhere, just you and me,
To a tropical island, resort, or sandy beach,
I could just see us, walking hand in hand with the hot sand
 beneath our feet,
On an island, just you and I, now wouldn't that be neat?

Anything we'd need would be right there,
You could watch the wind blow through my lovely hair,
And then we could look into each others eyes and see the
 ocean's waves,
I really would like to one of these days.

I could lay in your lap, and you could fill my face with
 your kisses,
And you would be fulfilling all my wishes.
We could picnic and have fun together,
I could lay there with you forever.

This day is about to come to an end,
But we will be back, you just say when.
I hope this dream someday comes true,
I really would like to, one of these days with you.

Have You Ever

Have you ever loved someone so much that it made you cry
But never told them the real reasons why?
Have you ever wanted to be with them but couldn't find the words to say
But when you got a chance, the words went away?

Have you ever wanted to call them up to just shoot the breeze
But when they said "hello," you would fall to your knees.
Have you ever seen them from a long distance away
And said under your breath, "I love you" anyway?

Have you ever sat down beside them, and accidentally touched their hand
And looked at them and smiled, as if you were in wonderland?
Have you ever looked into their eyes and wished they could read your mind?
The words you wanted to say—it wasn't the right time.

I know how it feels to feel this way.
And I hope to get over these mixed emotions one day.

This is how I feel when I'm with you,
Have you ever wanted to tell someone I love you?

Yes, I Have Always Wished For

Yes, I've always wished for someone just like you,
Who cares for, loves me, the way you do,
You are a very important person, you're the love of my life,
And one day I want to be your loving wife.

Yes, I want you and I to be together,
Together we both should be forever and ever.
Just you and I, together in love and in peace,
Yes, I've always wished one day that's the way it will be.

I'm glad some of my wishes have already come true,
And I'm glad someone loves me the way you do,
Yes, I've wished for a special friend, and that special friend
  is you,
Now together we can make the rest of my wishes come true.

Face-To-Face

You said you wanted to talk to me, face-to-face,
So we will go somewhere, just you and I, to a quiet place.
We will sit down and talk about our future and our past,
Fact-to-face, you and I, alone at last.

Face-to-face is where I want to be with you,
And I hope you feel the same way too,
We have been longing to be together,
I wish this talk could last forever,

I want to know how you feel about me in every way,
Don't be afraid, say what you have to say,
Just stand toe-to-toe and look me straight in my eyes,
If you love me, then tell me, please don't be shy.

But I'm not afraid to say what's on my mind,
Yes, I love you, once, twice, even a hundred times.
Time is pressures, to the both of us, and something we
   must not waste.
So let's take advantage of this time we have face-to-face.

Best Friends

When I first meet a person, I can usually sense a unique personality,
And God has given us a chance to finally meet,
A unique personality is very hard to find, no matter how hard you look,
A person is born with uniqueness, one can't get it by reading a book.

Whenever one meets another with this very special gift,
It will quickly give your heart and soul a lift,
To know one can communicate with another on the same wave links,
And who can comprehend on whatever each other thinks.

When best friends talk on any subject, they find peace of mind,
And when best friends tell secrets, honesty and trust they will find.
No matter when one needs a friend, they will always be right there,
And if one has a heavy burden, a friend will help another to bare.

When one finds someone with a unique gift of this kind,
Because truly the most precious gift is that of the mind,
By the many ways it makes one think, and how one manipulates,
One will always focus the mind on love and never hate.

You, my good friend, have a very unique personality,
And I'm glad we had a chance in this lifetime to meet,
Because to have a good friend in these days is very rare,
In this good-friend relationship, we will instill love and care.

This friendship was brought together by the good Lord
   up above,
And through His good grace, we will forever spread plenty
   of warmth and love,
This is the beginning of a very unique relationship between
   two friends,
And with the blessing from God, it will never never end.

This Time

This time it will be different, just you wait and see,
This time love will be right between you and me,
We've had our ups and downs in the past,
We've even been to the place where we didn't think it
  would last,

But this time things will be different, my head is now
  on straight,
For me to love another it is much too late,
For there is no other in this world for me than you,
Not being in love with you—what would I do!

I would be so lost, somewhere out in space,
While thinking only of your smiling face,
Things will be different, I know what I want this time,
I will think with my emotions and with my mind,

I'm ready to do the things I've for so long wanted to do,
Just give me your heart, and I'll be true to you,
My heart is already yours until the end of time,
For you and I, things will be different this time!

Your Smiling Face

It's very good to see you back in the swing of things
To see your smiling face sure makes my heart sing
To know you're on the road to recovery and a clean bill
 of health,
Let taking one day at a time be your first step.

Remember to take a break several times each day
And eat all the right foods, as each day passes away
You must put your hand in God's and He will see
 you through,
And always remember, He loves you.

Keep your bright smile, which will light up any place
And never stop bringing the smiles to the children's face.
And with God's grace, every step you take will get easier
 each day
And closer to His loving heart you will always stay.

So don't be in a hurry to get your school work done
Because all work and no play is no fun,
I will pray you may have many more steps to take
And I will never forget the warm and friendly smile on
 your face.

Love is Not Enough

And how my heart feels like salt in an open wound,
I look up to Heaven and say, "why me?"
If love is not enough, please Lord, make me see,

The things you have in store for our future to come
We must keep the faith and remain as one
Although the mountain is high and the valleys are low,
The Lord will follow in our footsteps wherever we go

Communication is a must, it's easier said than done
I want this relationship to remain as one
I've put feeling into it, I didn't know I had,
And I don't want to give up on the best thing I've ever had

You mean more to me, than the word "love" itself,
My love grows deeper for you than anyone else
I can't think past tomorrow without you by my side,
I want you near me, as my lover and my guide

These words I speak, from my heart to pen and pad,
This love is real, unlike any other I've ever had
Give me a chance to prove my love is real, as real as real
  can be
This is the one and only chance I want you to give me.

Have I Told You Lately I Love You

Have I told you lately I love you?
Without you in my life what will I do
I now we've been through ups and downs
And we've always managed to come around

There are so many things I wanted to say
I love you, in each and every way
Although I know I don't say these words much
When you look into my eyes I get a deep-down touch

I know it's been hard, but we must try
To get our life back together instead of saying goodbye
I feel your love by the way you look at me
I know there's something good in me, you see

I just want it to be like it used to be
Me loving you and you loving me
Please don't make me live this life without you
Have I told you lately I love you?

There Comes a Time

There comes a time, in every one's life, when they have to let go,
To a special bond, and those special memories of a special someone loved so
Yet your heart is torn, and the only real cure is time, it will mend it
Because the love which was once so strong now has ended.

There comes a time in everyone's life when they must smile to keep from crying
Because the relationship they once had is slowly dying
You will often think about the special memories shared together
Those memories will never fade away; they will last forever and ever.

There comes a time in everyone's life, when just the thought of living is no more
Because that special someone walks out the door
Don't let these things get you down—just keep a positive mind
And you will meet another special someone when there comes a time.

I'm Hurting Inside

I'm hurting inside, because I'm still in love with the one
 person for whom I care so much
My eyes are something closed, but when they reopen, there
 they are,
I find myself wandering somewhere out in space,
As tears of sadness roll down my face.

It hurts inside just to know we could never be as one again,
My love was strong, and very real, maybe that's why our love
 came to an end,
But I know now I could never love another without
 hurting inside,
And I will always love that special someone, and the hurt I
 cannot hide.

Maybe this is a test to see if I can stand the situations life has
 in store,
I will never be able to love another like the first love
 anymore,
I'm still wishing on that star, which is shining so very bright,
And I hope everything will be all right.

Time should cure old wounds, and maybe what I need
 is time,
To get myself back together and straighten out my mind.
I'm hurting inside, but someday that hurt will end,
And I can fall in love all over again.

If Our Love Was Meant to Be

The last several months have been hard for us to bear,
And life isn't promising to anyone to be fair,
Just because the world wants it to be.

Life is an experience and a true reality.
Each day we think about one another without saying a word,
Hoping and praying our thoughts could be heard,
Praying the other would break the ice or make the first move,
Cause the best love we ever had we didn't want to lose.

We often think back to love at first sight.
Hoping someday soon the other would hold them tight,
Closing your eyes each night, praying to Heaven above,
Knowing we will one day be able to give our love.

We often think of things to say when we're apart,
Never sharing our thoughts, when we're together, of
  the heart,
Wishing the other would speak soft words of some kind,
Thinking if only you could turn back the time.

Hoping one day we would be as one again,
And praying the bad dreams would come to an end,
We must open our hearts to what we feel,
And show each other every day our love is real.

I know this won't resolve in one day,
But we must start now, by making a way,
By talking and sharing, in our daily tasks,
Then our newly found relationship will truly last.

I know things have changed for you and for me,
Maybe by helping each other, we both can see,
If I'm right for you, and if your right for me,
Or if our love was ever meant to be.

For the Two of You to Share

This wedding remembrance was written just for you,
I know of no other couple with the love and respect of
   you two,
From the first moment we met, you have never changed
   a thing,
And the love I see in your eyes truly makes my heart sing.

To know two special people who give so much love,
Love is a great gift from Heaven above,
May you keep this very special gift as each day passes away,
And keep your hands in God's hand each and every day.

I know you will remember this moment until the end of time,
And may your next ten years bring you joy, happiness, and
   peace of mind,
To two very special people, there is one other thing I would
   like to say,
Keep on loving every day in every loving way.

I love you.
May God bless you.

The Cotton Field

Early one morning, before I start working in the cotton field
As I stand with my hand in my cotton sack, leaning on a
  wagon wheel
I raise my weary eyes up to heaven above
Thank my almighty God for spreading His precious love.

As the families pick cotton on a very hot summer day
They sing old hymns just to pass the time away
The more cotton they pick, the more baskets they have to fill,
And if they refuse they will have to answer to Master Bill.

For you know he owns them, the land, and the homes too
But they will keep praying to God, and He will see them
  through
Now the sun is going down, and the fall of night will come
As the families leave the cotton field they sing one day a
change will come.

The Desert Floor

As I look out over the desert floor, as far as I can see,
The big blue sky and the bright sunlight is shining down
   on me.
At the bottom of the mountain is where I lay,
As I look up into the sky, I see buzzards stalking their prey.

And on every round they get lower and lower,
As they wait for some helpless animal to die upon the
   desert floor.
I can see a coyote out of the corner of my eye,
As he stalks a small bird as it passes by.

There I can see a lake going dry, just a few feet away,
And all that's left is a bed of dy clay;
The rocks and the sand, they both sparkle in the sunlight,
As I look in the cactus tree, a new mother gives her little ones
   a bit.

The sun is going down over the hills and the mountain tops
   on this calm sunny day;
And a very warm feeling came over me.
As I lay in the desert sun and look up to Heaven above,
Thanking God for allowing me to see Him spread His
   Precious Love.

To the Athlete

This is only the beginning of the race for you,
And there are many other things in your minds you must do.
So don't get uptight and stop running this race,
Because there are many more obstacles in the world you
    must face.

When things get tough, as they sometimes will,
Please don't take drugs, because drugs will kill.
They are supposed to make you feel good, before or after
    you play,
But you may not be around to talk about them the next day.

It's hard enough in this world just to stay alive,
So please don't drink and drive.
Take it from me, I'm an athlete,
If you do drugs, you will surely be beat!

Creative Arts in Learning

C- reative arts in learning has a very unique philosophy
R- enewing your spirits and enhancing your teaching simultaneously
E- ffective teaching strategies and a variety of teaching techniques
A- rts teach about cultural diversity, each and every angle they will meet
T- he arts touch the heart, free the spirit, and address human development
I- mprove your self-esteem and also self-confidence
V- arious intelligence including kinesthetic, spatial, music, verbal, interpersonal, and interpersonal too
E- nhance your cognitive skills, such as symbol formation, organizing, and applying an old solution to problems that are new

A- rt provides an avenue for people of all ages alike
R- elationships which are healthy and appreciative of differences of all types
T- he arts help a child learn important lessons about himself
S- uch as self-discipline, persistence, self-esteem, and a sense of personal wealth

I- nsight into a whole world of teaching creativity
N- ew aspects of skilled abilities through new diversity

L- evel of sheer survival and mastery of learning styles and skills
E- xperiment with new discoveries and the turning of your creativity wheel
A- rtist, dancers, poets within will blossom like a rose
R- ediscovering a new opportunity for each to unfold
N- o one knows what the future holds, so be all that you can be
I- nvest into a brand new world of growth and creativity
N- o specific arts background is required in any way
G- o ahead, make the first move towards your future in creative arts in learning today.

A Montessori Child Is the Future of Tomorrow

M- ontessori method is to help a child in the early years of life to master skills,
O- f the brain, of body language, to get the turning of the wheels,
N- in life of his first two-and-a-half to six years,
T- o be transformed into a tool of art and creations.
E- arly education of a child is essential for all generations.
S- pecific goals are achieved, directed by the brain,
S- kills such as sound from a mere organ he will gain,
O- nce he has developed these impressions, he will be able to communicate.
R- evealing his hidden talent, developing personality and other traits,
I- t educates him with knowledge and enriches him as a whole.

M- ethods he will need to fulfill his future goals,
E- xploring his environment, culture, and, most of all, his potentials.
T- o lead to the formation of man and his own personality,
H- umanity he will gain, making the world a brighter place,
O- pening the door which holds the key to hope for the future.
D- irect your child's future, make him a Montessori child.

I Quit

At the end of my day, this is how I feel
My toes hurt, my head aches. I need a pill
The students won't stop talking or playing so I can speak
I'm glad this is the last hour and the last day of the week

The names are on the board of those who broke the rules
Because they came to class today just to act like fools
Now my head is aching, and my feet are too
I can't think straight; what shall I do

The assignment I gave them they didn't turn them in
Can someone please tell me when will all this madness end—
So, if I don't fit don't force it, just relax and let it go
That's why *I Quit* and I won't be back tomorrow

If It Is to Be, It's Up to Me

Each of us has hopes and dreams we want to see come true,
Just keep believing in yourself, it's up to only you,
Be all you can be, because you truly are the best,
Special people like you deserve nothing less.

If it is to be, then it will take place,
And always remember to keep God in your life and His
    good grace
Because He is the key, which we all will need,
And all you have to do is believe

In yourself, and in your dreams too,
And always remember it is up to only you,
And then you can say someday, if it is to be,
It is truly up to me.

Physical Education Song, Repeat After Me

We're the kids from Cahlen School,
We always obey the school rules,
We like to run and have some fun,
Heart and muscles, they are strong.

Good health is the key each and every day,
Making us stronger as we work and play,
Now we are going to leave you with our motto,
And repeat it after me/us if you don't know.

If it is to be, it is up to me.
If it is to be, it is up to me.
(Repeat)

Sound off 1, 2.
Sound off 3, 4.
1-2-3-4!